The Breathing House

DATE DUE

DEMCO, INC. 38-2931

The Breathing House

✦

Imagist Poems

Marcielle Brandler

iUniverse, Inc.
New York Lincoln Shanghai

The Breathing House
Imagist Poems

iUniverse books may be ordered through booksellers or by contacting:

iUniverse
2021 Pine Lake Road, Suite 100
Lincoln, NE 68512
www.iuniverse.com
1-800-Authors (1-800-288-4677)

ISBN-13: 978-0-595-40408-7 (pbk)
ISBN-13: 978-0-595-84783-9 (ebk)
ISBN-10: 0-595-40408-1 (pbk)
ISBN-10: 0-595-84783-8 (ebk)

Printed in the United States of America

Contents

Acknowledgements

Acknowledgements are made to the following publications in which these poems have appeared:

As You Requested, a chapbook produced by Marcielle Brandler, "America: At Your Service," "The Civilian, The Siege," "April Third: On the Street," new title is "On the Street," "Koyaanisquatsi," and "The Request,"1986.
California Poets in the School: Los Angeles Poets Anthology, "Monroe, Utah," Fall 1995.
Corners Magazine: an Assemblage of Poems by the Pasadena Poets, "The Civilian, The Siege," and "the Request," 1985.
Disclosure. Voices of Women, New Alliance Records: "The Civilian The Siege." 1992.
Eclipse: "Lark in the High Desert." 2003
Haight Ashbury Literary Journal: "I Met a Man."
Hurākan: "Raven's Canyon." 1995.
Moment Magazine, "April 3: On the Street," New title "On the Street," 1987.
Poems by the Gifted Students, a chapbook of the students at Glenwood Elementary School, and for California Poets in the Schools, produced by Marcielle Brandler, "Frolic," 1989.
Revista:Review Interamericana, University of Puerto Rico, "Lark in the High Desert," and "The Breathing House," 1994.
Shrinking Chants, a chapbook produced by Marcielle Brandler, "Ituri Forest," "Koyaanisquatsi," "To Lightnin Hopkins' Blues," "America: At Your Service," "Two Beauties," "Experience and Art," "The Civilian, The Siege," "These Are the Words," 1990.
Southern California Anthology: "Monroe, Utah,." 1995.
The Forum: "America: At Your Service", "Inner Café," and "Paladins of the Styx." 1997.
Two Twenty-four Poetry Quarterly: "Black School."
Voices. New Poems of Life and Experience: "Inner Café," 1994.
Wilderness of Dreams: California Poets in the Schools Statewide Anthology, "Eden," 1998.

"Eden" and "The Senator Remembers the Lobbyist," *Arts and Letters*, Summer 2005.

"Inner Café," "The Request," and "Frolic," *Arts and Letters*, Fall 2005.

"Eden" won First Prize for the Mount San Antonio College 25th Annual Writers' Conference, 1997.

Special Thanks

I wish to express my gratitude to poet/screenwriter, James Ragan whose encouragement kept me clear about what writing means to me, and whose magnanimous contributions of time and guidance as mentor are deeply appreciated. Thanks to Eduardo Kotliroff, for whisking me away to locations in Brazil and Argentina, featured in some of these poems.

Years ago, Denise Levertov critiqued a few of these poems at the request of my dear mentor, Professor Vladimir Ussachevsky, electronic music composer/pioneer, who is now deceased. Posthumous thanks to him. Vladimir was a great inspiration and loved by many. I wish also to thank poet, William Matthews for his help with this manuscript. Unfortunately, Bill is no longer with us. His generosity and gentle spirit will never be forgotten.

Many thanks to Jack Hirschman who inspired me to publish my chapbooks and organize my reading series with Marc Colasurdo in the early eighties. We called it Urban Mobile Poets, and we read poetry all over California inviting dancers, musicians, actors, and other poets to perform with us.

I would like to add to this list, my friend, Lionel Rolfe, who pushed me to reorganize these poems and get this book out to the world. Finally, to poet, Dave Smith, who, when I was an undergraduate in 1974, told me that none of the first manuscript I gave him were poems, except a line of mine which read, "Our lips were hot." Now I understand.

Thank you all for your gracious attentions!

I would like to thank the people who gave donations to the publishing of this book. They are:

Allen Donesh, my student
Evelyn Pizano, my student
Doris Allen, my friend
Chris Peditto, friend and publisher of Heat Press

Maria Royce, my friend
Bradney Borg and Danielle Muir, my nephew and sweetheart for their
generous donation
Janet Bennett., my friend
Curtis England, my student

And special thanks to Rick Mizuno, friend and author of 50/50 Split, published
by iUniverse, for his very generous donation. I also thank Rick for urging me to
publish with iUniverse. Thanks to Connie Russell, my Publishing Service Associate, for all her wonderful help and to Phil Whitmarsh for his guidance even
before I sent in my manuscript.

Introduction

Poetry saves lives. Poetry comforts. During the tragedies of 9/11, radio news reporters said that people were calling the station, asking for poetry. Short stories, comedy, and other forms of entertainment were not appropriate. They could not conquer the deep feelings of loss this country suffered. People reportedly were dusting off old books of poetry and turning to them for solace—for answers.

Poetry gives many of us, who do not fit into society's usual definition of normalcy, a place to call our own. We are all poets, you and I. If you feel, then you are a poet, whether you write or not.

My poetry emerges from the deepest levels of anguish—not only my pain, but the sorrow I intuit from humanity's struggle—to the dizzying heights of sheer joy. I often cry in the presence of great beauty. When I hear Samuel Barber's Adagio for Strings or political songs of various peoples, I am deeply moved. When I see individuals of different cultures or backgrounds cooperating for a common goal, I weep for the beauty of it.

I give myself permission to FEEL. In seminars for all ages, that is the first thing I teach writers: Allow yourself to feel and to express those feelings. I understand their struggle to express. We have been taught to be quiet and listen, while our elders emote and lecture. We are taught that our thoughts and feelings are not valuable and will not make us a living. When I was very young, I felt old because of my suffering, I wrote poems and songs. My dreams were operas. They were sexy and mysterious. I felt complicated, powerful yearnings, and I was very conscious that I did not have the vocabulary to express those amazing thoughts.

Now, I am fully grown and know how to say what I feel. What happens in "Eden" is a true story. My mother was very beautiful and cruel. She expressed only disdain for me. Poems like "The Civilian, The Siege" and "America: At Your Service" came directly from my political involvement helping refugees. "Inner Café" was written when loneliness drove me mad. In those days, there was always a man waiting in the wings, but he was never the one I loved.

Many of my poems come to me all in one frenzied moment of writing and have never been rewritten. Often, I would wake at four am, write, and return to dreamland. Because I was a singer/songwriter, my poems tend to be rhythmic. I have worked with dancers who danced my poems, musicians who interpreted my poems, other poets and actors who created performance pieces with the work we both wrote. We did benefits for the homeless, for the literacy campaign, and many others. I wrote rap poetry in the early eighties, before it became popular, and throughout it all, I have met amazing artists from all stripes. They are regular people who have found forms in which to express themselves. Poetry is not just for the elite. Poetry is for everyone.

EDEN

I startled my mother in the blazing
hallway, her breasts an exotic gift
my lips had never suckled. It was

an accident we met. Never before
had I beheld anyone naked. My sisters
told me of the times they had watched

her. I imagine my mother lifting
herself from the forgiving floral suds
of her bath. This secret time I had

never visualized until now. She glides
on her hose, attaching them with
little posy snaps, and perfumes

herself in her personal
scent. Slithering into her
strapless cocktail dress, her

shoulders glowing, she fluffs up
her hair like a delicate fern,
then entwines the glittering

necklace and presses on the blossom
lipstick which my father will kiss
from her mouth before they

lie down in the room where only they
may sleep. What are these angry wings
barring me from her garden? I remember

the last time she bathed me. I was
five and embarrassed. I turned away,
and she left me in my
unscented water.

PRAGUE

And the drift
Of the sing
In cobblestone colors

Pierce my heart
The love-city
The city-bridge

The bridge of cities
Binding the artists
To their places

Palettes spinning o're
The heads of schoolchildren
Their uniforms crisp

And windy. Cafes packed
With Americans, with
Germans. If post

Office workers refuse
To help you, you must
Learn more Czech.

Where are the writers?
Tourists celebrate dead
Artists. The prostitute in

Wensleslaw Square dances
For the poorest gypsy
I ever saw. No cats.

No dogs. Just swarms
Of people touring, studying,
Snapping cameras.

Snapping bits of memory
From pieces of Prague
To hustle home.

BLACK STAGE

Someone has called
the red leaves home.
Scriptures in the sky
are peeling down.

My sisters rake and burn
them with unspoken fires,
while I lounge with my aged

parents on the porch and wait
for the first stars.
My mother has mesmerized us

with their transmissions like
the saga she invented
of why my half-brother was banished

from us when he was only nine,
and why we were forbidden, all our
years, to speak his name. Mother

defines the sparks searing through
Orion. I search the black hole,
the antimatter of her eyes.

My sisters point to the frayed
landscape of our lives
and the evidence above us.

Someone has seen us
gawking. Someone
is pulling it all away.

NINE-FOOT TALL GRIZZLY

He has come too close for the range
of my binoculars. I have twisted
the lenses for closer, closer. Then
I see him without them. The sheen

off his square back confuses my eyes.
He hurls a trout into the air,
chases it flopping upstream. I remain
breathless behind this granite as he

hunkers around in a circle, his nose
snorting the water. He rinses the
scales from his paws. They glisten
like coins to his elbows. Then,
inexplicably he rises bellowing,
to his full nine feet and looms on
his haunches. Water falls off
his nails. He wades up the bank.
He shakes down a pine tree

and snaps it in half. Falling
like a child with pudgy legs
extended, he sits and scrapes
away the bark, and licks up

the evacuating termites. But,
just now, he stops short, gives
the air a great sniff. He has
caught my scent. I do not know

what my next move should be as
a visitor who sits beyond
the footlights watching
this Chumash medicine man dance.

THE SENATOR SPEAKS OF THE LOBBYIST

He leads me to an anteroom.
He shows me the slick publication
of spliced photographs.
At the buffet table, a perplexing
vigor bursts from his eyes.

On the dance floor, he presses
his hips to mine,
and the coil of hundred dollar
bills excites my anticipation,
as it does every time we embrace.

He is able to play along when I
clasp his hand, keeping my
noncommittal distance,
reticent to kiss-kiss for the cameras.

We have discussed the jeopardy
of free speech as situations and
power bases reverse themselves.

Now those once in
power serve the new
power

RAVEN'S CANYON
(For Eduardo)

Your fingers in. The robe
draped across insinuations.
Where does the raven fly
who leaps off our pinnacle?

You skim canyon from my scales.
Warm in your wings, I lie
feathered. I chant as my
people do:

> Beauty before me
> Beauty behind me
> Beauty all around me
> I walk in beauty.

Night zephyr whips metallic
shadows and scrapes the mesas.
The screeching excites us in
our smallness, we who stand
among dainty stones with
elongated silhouettes, our wet
hair slapping around our heads,
our shirts billowing open.

All things are dwarfed against
the rock walls. Coyotes lope
towards a cave near our motel.
Feathers on a truck antennae
flip like a dry butterfly.
I suck on my awe and hold
your silver shadow in mine.

BLACK SCHOOL

From my windy heart
I watch as the imagist nun
kneels a pose
for the students she rules.

The schoolyard weeps
its smog on the shrieking
black girls this last day.
Careless teens jig and bob

in the circle we make.
Gossip stings the wilting
teachers who smile bitterly
to their paychecking ends.

They applaud their Sister
Lupe's moves and glare
at the newcomer who dances
with a Catholic chalice

THE BREATHING HOUSE

Two breasts appear next
to my cheek as I sleep.
They have been waiting
among bluebirds and mothers
who died in childbirth, waiting
like a pasture of mustard plants,
to immerse me in the anonymity
of nighttime clouds. I rise
and stand before this dream
to decide its future.

I am delirious
with its airbrushed eight-foot lady,
Indians woven into the woodwork
of a fence, a pink cement truck
dragging a plug along the dry grass
like a morning horse. I undress
floating in the wind and swim
to the nape of the ocean in search of
the other side of its horizon.

TO LIGHTNIN HOPKINS' BLUES

Oh Lightman, oh Lightman.
You swing in that hammock.
You singin' that bluesome,

and jam that guitar.
Oh, jam that guitar.

This ol' record's worn out.
Your soul's still got fingers

to play those ol' riffs, Man,
to slide down a tune.

Ah, hell, who can swing me
a story like you?

Who rode on that train
with my daddy, the hobo?

Sing me some charcoal.
Fly by my grapes.

Say it's alright,
and I'll try it again,

cuz somehow you said it,
what can't be just spoke.

Say we be tight,
and we'll try it again.
Lightnin.

TWO BEAUTIES

Veils of leaf screen
the grace of a deer
cracking pine needles
where he prances.

No stranger to startled
birds warbling
as they dart
through the mist.

Chase over. Percussive
from rushes on rock.
Spring fancy,
fleet hollow,
and bounce.

See the stag
turns his throat
to the cool
mountain rain,
and the eye
always sees
beyond reach.

While inside
a green cabin
wearing loose
cotton robes
walks a silhouette
waving in light.

As she bends
near a trunk,
the lid creaking
in dust, stretching
dry spider webs
'til they snap.

And the lady
hums high,
as the breeze
takes a ride
through the cloud
of her hair
brightly feathering.

Slowly, Deborah's hand
sliding flesh over brass.
there she lifts
out a dress
worn for traveling.

DECISION

A puff of gray anger
when you see the
loose hair of that
other woman over
your lover's eye.
A smell ejects you
from the present
taking you back
many years.

For me it's

crab grass cut, the train whistle,
and knotted alley cats who moan
on fences which grip the white
field surrounded by eucalyptus
saplings, collies and shepherds
rambling in days of friendly
dogs escorting us children on
adventures in raw meadows where

war vet hobos, or their illusions,
left army blankets and cans in
the basement hold of a demolished
house with one wall that refused
to lie down. Freckled, tanned
neighbor boys waved the caboose,
tiptoed in sticker patches as
the train clanked by.

For a time I

forget the indecision
of my man and how
I wait on his love
and how I have
abandoned all others.

INNER CAFE

An iguana gulps
a cube of melting light
and pops like a firecracker.
Two window panes go
skywriting by.
A wooden whistle snaps.
White twigs fly
at my face and drop
past the pillars
in the moviehouse.

I rise leaving
needle-pricks of longing
stuck in the armchair.
The stranger near me
eating mystery
does not see sighs
like dust trailing
from the lace
of my shadow.
I shall not ignite
the man who waits for me.

THE CIVILIAN
THE SIEGE

She opens in front of the mirror.

> Bomb waits.

She rides the door.

> Leaves grow legs.

She crumples the letter which smells
of leaves.

> Gunners pump.

She throws her red dress into the fire.

> A bandage drips in bush.

She pulls a proxy on top of her.

> A mouth kisses a rifle butt.

She screams, goes limp.

> A brain crawls out of its skull.

> Her lovers go off.

SO HE FOUGHT IN A WAR
(For Bruce Weigl and Remembering John)

I rock with a smile
his gray illusions into the deep.

He is the one whose whiskers
have stiffened. I am the one

he scrapes with his
fevered jolt.

Mine is the hair hangs
over his face, his eyes aching

inwards. His speech crawls
along our sheets. His hand-to-hand

dramas enrich his tears.
He counts those tears,

pulls them back like marbles
for his pouch,

and re-uses them, over
and over and under and in.

The lovers of his life are
a nameless strand. I count their

colors and smells like stained
recipes left in a bombed-out

kitchen. He uses us like
incestuous sisters.

WHAT THE UGLY BOY AND THE PRETTY GIRL HAVE IN COMMON

She is stared at.

His face is passed over.

Neither of them

are seen.

She's so cute, it's assumed
she's spoiled.

He's so ugly, he's cute.

He can't believe she likes him.

She's afraid he'll find something
he doesn't like.

They marry.
Over the years,
his face acquires dignity,

and her face gains
character.

Now, people say
how

alike they look.

WHEN I USED TO DRIVE THE FAST LANE

I thought it would be easiest,
would get me there fastest,
but I kept getting lost.
The oncoming lights blinded me.

The debris from other failures
always slowed me up. So many
times, I took the wrong road
and found I couldn't get off.

So many faces behind speeding
walls and windows. I thought
I could see. So many eyes in
my rear-view mirror; someone

I could have loved, someone
who thought wrongly of me,
someone I thought I wanted,
someone who broke me

down and left me stranded.
I wanted to make these happy
times with a song that would
blast to the others. But they

were bouncing to their own
tunes or chatting on their own
phones, barely aware of
the road. There I was, more

alone by searching than if
I'd never gone out

KOYAANISQUATSI
A Hopi word from the film title meaning, "Life out of balance"

Breakers of mist climb
boulders of cloud and hurdle
through white gasps.

Sea of sky meanders like fur.
Restless monoliths of whispers.
Mountains disperse into birds.
Canyons like the open mouth
of a seventy-thousand-foot lion.
No hyena calls louder than this
silence.

A cupboard slams.
A curb rams a car.
Thirty-five-story buildings
with shredded eyes buckle
like elephants to their knees.

Ton trucks.
Snout to tail.
Snout to tail.
Derricks send coils
through the earth.
Satellites whisk around
its axis.

Terrorists and peasants bleed
into the soil. Presidents
and plumbers sleep

in coffins. Newscasters'
nightmares are washed
down the drain with
the toothpaste.

Opera stars shatter lovers.
Dealers shatter cocaine bricks.
People in lines pop
through subways and
sift into subcars along
subtracks, out subcars,
out subways and back
in again. Nine to five,
ten to three, twelve
priests, twelve planets,
twelve applicants.

The undertow of evolution
from grunts to bustles
to shaved rats on
diamond-studded chains
to the female man.

We are the bodies in
the body. Hatchets,
projectiles, and the
globe splits from
the pounding.
The core screams.
Core spits.

Volcanoes
rise from the waters
and crack through
metropolis sidewalks.
their fiendish maxophones
turn on themselves.
I must adore you quickly.

SILVERLAKE

Dust in the dips
between five freeways,
between someone's
injured dog.

Dog fight.
And someone means
all who live here.

All in crack'd houses,
who stroll past
the lake with its

evening lilies and
hobos and fugitives
and scribbling gangs.

Mexican couples in
the foot-pushing boats.
Whites in artistic,

boarding-house channels
of jazz fusion and left-
wing decisions. Dislocated

theatres with X or Sex
on the front. Puddles
of black and brown

where the Burbank white
and the powder blue
and the Pasadena Jesus

freaks would never venture
to the chipped paint
and primitive cats.

Cats with complicated
relationships. The calico
is the friend of the cat-in-law

of the sexiest female
within five blocks, and she
is the best huntress, leaving
her master a headless bird
outside his room once in
awhile.

Fear is not the issue,
but eviction or car theft,
or…. Well, that's

another matter.
After all, this is not
Redondo beach, but

a guy with a window
sign just drove by.
"I love my wife."

And everyone does
get a free left turn
at the signal, even
if it is toward the
City of Industry.

HOTEL CHANCE

Think of the sum of
potentialities when a single
woman looks to a man, his
green eyes, her black hair
in their children. His money
would make her stories real.
His body would give her
body reason to bask. Each
is a city, politicking
the other city, exploiting
its resources. The man has

his bags always packed.
The woman rejoices beneath
his waterfalls wondering if
the man will stay. He
is a seed in the vast
bed of her longing. As
she gazes at him, she
wonders, "Have the gods
inscribed my struggle
carefully, or am I left

to scribble in some last-
minute fate?" The woman
rolls to touch the muscle
of her lover's chest. His
sleep has taken him from
her. Their bed has cried
its last, and she rises
taking with her no memento,
no provisions. When the man
wakes, will he wonder what
he is liberated from?

ON THE STREET

Just now a stubbly
bum stood behind

me under a tree by
the curb.

    I got up to walk
    away.

He knew I snubbed
his presence

    He said,

"That's alright. You
don't have to
go. I'm
going."

    I knew it made
    him sad, but I

just kept on
walking

without

looking at him

without

a word.

    Where did I learn

that?

AMERICA: AT YOUR SERVICE

Over the table she leans.
Her breath chills in the glasses
And drops on the ice.
Mugs like burners on a stove.

The baritone across the pancakes.
To her, he's a mountain.
Does it mean a green card?
Love? A new dress?
Will she cash it in for

Half-American babies?
For legal documents?
Will she never go home?
Does home exist anymore?

PENAL COLONY
(To Lovers, to Writers in Prisons, and to Elio)

I have been exiled to this desert.
I have been instructed to freeze.
My lover has been taken from me.

The sentry's pearl knuckles clutch
around the keys. We speak only of
the heat, the cold; never of our views.

I watch silhouettes circling on
the periphery of prison. They sharpen, fade.
Clattering night makes vague gestures.

I know it is hopeless to call to the shadows.
If we are brought together, they will be
taken from me to increase my despair.

Twelve days ago, I was visited. They said
it was my friend. It was my lover. Perhaps
they do not know who we are to one another.

Perhaps they do. Because of this, we did not
touch. Because of this, I could not tell if
he loved me. All my yearnings were mocked

by moments we spent speaking riddles, my
anticipations for ecstasy denied. Yesterday,
the guard repeated what I had mumbled in my

sleep and asked what it meant. I lied saying
I did not know. He showed me a photo of his
children and asked again. He poured me wine.

He watched my averted eyes. I said
nothing. Tomorrow, I will write on
the wall, words I have not yet conceived

before I escape this dead romance.

HOW THE LOVERS RUSH

How the lovers rush
to one another's arms
after long separation.
A glance is bittersweet
before the first touch.

Horatio!
Our velvet green boy
suckling in the theater,
reminds the dying painter
of his own yearnings,
reminds me of valleys

I stood above in the good dream,
a gargantuan poem
written upon the graveyards
of every country superseding
the collective chatter

of ten billion spirits. Yet,
my love is like all others.
You swell in my mouth,
whipped cream, champagne.
We are akin to water

Scorpions, flicking like one
organism, each so miniscule.
We dye the water red,
and it is impossible to
decipher the individuals.

THE GESTAPO

Soul? Who can think of this
when
hip-two-three slap-load-kick
stop outside your house?

Who has time to consider Honor
when the door flies in and
your housemate is escorted away?

You lie pulsing on your bed
with your running shoes tight
and a sloshing canteen
hugged to your stomach.

You practice a code
before every phone call.
"Hi. It's me, down-the-road.
You know, up-the-street?"

Your garden has been
harvested too soon.
You start drying dishes
to give you a reason
to stand by the window.

You break more glasses.
You stop drinking
wine with dinner.
The radio is always talking,
and you have stopped talking.

You forget to eat.
You stop paying bills.
You
Stop.

PRAYER DEN IN SÃO PAULO

Descending the steps of the little church
beneath the black god the Catholics call
Saint Antonio de Catigeno, we fold
our hands and stoop like devotees.

A shaking man massages his fingers.
He pushes a coin at the vendor and takes,
from the glass case, a five-foot candle.
He adjusts it like a shovel, then softens
down into the heat. Behind him,
we enter a charred dungeon

with moats along four walls. Tapers drip
in the canals, melting wax splays upon the water.
A man in blue jeans scoops cooled drippings,
with his fingers, like abandoned prayers,
and tosses them over
his head into a rusted coffee can.

Out a block of window, I can see
the feet of passersby. Candles, like steeples
six feet tall, are propped in an iron stand. Wax
grows moldy along their sides.

Purple illusions rise in the flames, rise
in the murmurs uttered by the man next
to me in his suit cut from another
century. I waver, nearly fainting. For relief,
we climb the stairs to the street.

I look at the drawn people shuffling by
in this city, drained of hope and color and
even longing. The chapel above is a murky
ghost, its only bright spot the ornate red, gold,
and blue stained glass narrative of peasants agog at
the crowned serpent defiantly coiled around his pole.

I MET A MAN
(To Professor David Bennett)

I met a man
whose bones
illuminated
his body.

His skin
spread out
the light
and the blue

in his veins
wound like
blackberry
port.

BILINGUAL

Flood of my soul
christens the flesh
I am sent to inhabit.

Like a dormant cloud
charging with electricity,
I come to life.

Unlike a hermit crab
squeezing into a shell
on the ocean floor,

my soul's hydraulic
momentum forges a channel
to life's open sea.

My voice defines
the intimate moments
of our occupied mouths.

When tongue licks
air, it speaks two
ways.

Freedom Word.
Freedom Flesh.

LARK IN THE HIGH DESERT

I wade through echoes
in the spices of sand clouding
around my legs. It is enough
for me, a ghost, to wave
at the train and see it turn
to the blue ambivalence of powder.

The tape-looped drinking
songs of city-poor men
are stored in the needles
of Joshua trees. I have come
many miles to see an abandoned truck
cab rusting near a fallen shed.
Fishhook cacti announce their own
inevitability. In a field
of wild barley a woman swings
a scythe over the heads
of blonde, gaping stalks.

I am entering a small town
where memories argue like chickens.
I pass a library overgrown
with aromatic pennyroyal.

In the cemetery I embarrass a man
who is kneeling inside a grave
chanting Italian. He rehearses
a marriage proposal facing the light,
then stops. Into the crown
of broadleaf filigree,
a western meadowlark tumbles.

THE DAY THE EARTH STOOD STILL

The First Tower

I'm dialing
my wife.

An airplane
has crashed through
my office wall.

Two stockbrokers
are carrying a torn and
shivering secretary

to the defeated
staircase. The elevators
have sunken in-
to the shaft.

"Honey, Call these numbers,"
I say. They are of families
we have never met.

She tells them their loved ones
are safe. Executives,
clients, janitors
clamor toward the roof.

The fire department report
it's the safest place.
They return saying
The door is locked.

Just in case, I say,
"Honey, I love you. Tell
the kids, I love them."

Suddenly, a ball of fire.

DECONSTRUCTING MYSTERY
(To the Great Dancer, Pavlova)

My bare arms
reveal no joy
as joy would

have you
believe it
to be smiling.

The beams
which ride on
my shoulders

are inside.
If ballet
is inherent

in the forest,
one becomes
a forest

only to
intellectualize
trees.

EXPERIENCE AND ART
(To Composer, Vladimir Ussachevsky)

Pulls a sharp turn,
the body vehicle. You leap
off quantum byways, spin
boulders in algebraic orbits.
You are a splinterflash
from cracked cliffs,
sideswiping the ears

of copperheads and mountain
lions. Sweltering breasts
of the mountains compel
the valley to hum
beneath the great wheel
of your trundling intention.
Your swelling heart aches

to fill the canyon, pumping
dilating like a new planet
expanding in the void.
You rise from yourself
like a spaceman, buoyant,
launching from his ship.
Nature does not pose

for you. Between every
thread of canvas,
your fingerpaints fill
the spaces of geometric
chalklines. Soaking
of nature's verdancy
through pores of your
surface to enlarge

your innate matboard,
until, by calibrations,
its fresco becomes
Empyrean with cavemen
emerging from holes
like bees. Their clubs
are honey-filled scepters.

Your sinks contain the ponds
oceans splash into. Now,
you are the mural
man walks through.

MONROE, UTAH
(To My Parents)

As I, in my listening
to the slim bird's trust,
aware of the grasses
that introduce the hill,
aware of the lights
which are strung
in the towns and glad
here's a place
called Monroe.

I rise by my pulse.
Each adventure is played
to its end. The Setter
who chases the sheep,
the woman who chases
the dog, the stranger
who waves from a truck
leaving dust like spirits
to fall back to the ground.

A blue peacock roofing,
hangs his train down
the wall. Dancing
the creek, the white cock
screams. The cow tells
her story. I sense
the discussions of the herd.
On this salty land, I am
dust on the boughs
of stillness, rustled by
the gossip of roots.

WATCHING RIVER MOSS

Is it an old siren's hair?
Is it an underwater geisha's
hand curling, wrist rotating
around an eight ball across
a table of dunked proposals?

The mermaid's arms extend
above her head as she bows
at the waist and beckons
me to fall in. This is my
river, the place where the

upstream trout are sparring
and gazing past the surface
at finches who fly beyond
the bar to their partners
whistling in familial calm.

FROLIC

Footprints of children
after a day's sand hurling war.
The odor of their bodies
mixes with powdered shell
and burgeons their caricatures
through the mist.

Seashores of their voices foam
over waterlogs and jellyfish
as the limitless hand of water
curls to itself
and somewhere shuts its bottomless eye.

Dusk lowers its curtains.
The games are closed,
the discus hurled back to the gods.
The sea has gone home,
and high tides guard youth's entrances.

BURY ME IN MOJAVE

Face me up on
the reckless
chaparral
where spines
and sucker

plants absorb
my waters.
Let ant swill
to ant my
saline until

each soldier,
worker, queen
receives a
shimmy through
the craw of

its chatter.
I saturate
through their
communal
pheromone code.

I will wait
for teeth
and surge
my blood in
the throats

of coyotes'
songs when
the moon
cries down
my eyes.

Let snake
steal whispers
from my ear
on his
desolate path,

shedding his
necklace of
silver foil.
Let haggling
buzzards hear

no names,
scoop entrail
samples for
their stretching
young, and

muffle their
screeches. It
may be the only
way I rise above
bookish scorpions.

THE REQUEST

You asked me if I
would just stand still.

At first, I felt gangly
naked, gigantic, while

you knelt becoming
dwarfed. But your

breath on my feet
made the cold above

otherworldly.
My feet in the tropics.

My shoulders in a
snowstorm. Your tongue

rolling along my ankles,
my arch, sweeping me

downstream, through all
the tears I have

ever cried. You lead
me to my childhood.

The molten crystal
of a shot glass

over which you hugged
me and listened. Now

my legs listen
to your soft chest.

The swirl, your words
slaking through my knees,

an oval of French,
of satin ellipses.

The white gold
of your skin

blurs through your hair,
washing the nerves

in my neck as they
bless with fragrance.

Oh, the round breasts,
half man, almost woman,

which can only be adorned
by calling them your name.

Your hair against my mouth
fogs me past all the

histories I have knelt
through, past postures

and languages, learned
forgotten. Your outcry

is an oath twisting
in your muscles. Animals

on leaves. The terrible
burst of our ripe power,

digging for the life
inside one another

A double whirlwind
uniting our gusts,

crashing our storm.
The out of your cry

is lightning to
my panic. It has
burned down

my will pitted ·
against you,

has built up
our enravishment,

built up our
craving, built

up my reverence.
And in the silence

of last tremors,
we measure our

contentment, and
remember the hysteric.

If a moment can
disperse years,

then I can say, All
was worth surviving.

PALADINS OF THE STYX

The waters of the Underworld
finger our shores,
digging eventual trenches.

We visit that River in our sleep,
and upon subterranean lily pads
dance our lessons,
taught by ghouls and fairies.

We spy the reflections
of our reptilian faces
beneath the water's
humble surface,
inklings of who we were
before Earth came to be
and what we are
evolving towards.

The hemispheres of
Day, of Night, Conscious,
Subconscious, Birth,
Rebirth, Death, Re-death,

are Longitude Pale,
Latitude Eternal,
where the icy hand
is warmed only
after our arrival.

There, where no anchor
has dug in, the abyss
sucks away our dead
longings, the bodies
of what we thought
we would become.

I turn toward it, but
briefly, and gripping
myself to earth
where it is familiar.

That which is beyond
life seems vile,
because we cannot
know it without

surrendering. The core
of creation
pulls us down in, soaks
out our earth-bogged
anemic colors,
recharges our
blazing magnetism,
releases us to our
electrified power.

THESE ARE THE WORDS

Your body is a path
I climb.

Your humor,
a meadow for my rest.

Your childhood, a legend
I pull at your sleeve to hear.

Your days are knotted hands
I massage.

Your writings are oceans
I can only hold in handfuls.

Your eyes are languages
I study and rehearse.

978-0-595-40408-7
0-595-40408-1

Printed in the United States
67423LVS00007B/226-234

9 780595 404087